Mysteries of life

Told in five stories

you will never

forget

Leo R. Hunt

Mysteries of Life Told in Five Stories You Will Never Forget

Copyright © 2022 by Leo R. Hunt

All rights reserved. No part of this publication may be reproduced, distributed, or transmitted in any form or by any means, including photocopying, recording, or other electronic or mechanical methods, without the prior written permission of the publisher or author, except in the case of brief quotations embodied in critical reviews and certain other noncommercial uses permitted by copyright law.

ISBN: (Paperback) 978-1639454488
       (eBook)   978-1639454495

Writers' Branding Revised Date: 12/12/2022

The view expressed in this book are solely those of the author and do not necessarily reflect the views of the publisher, and the publisher hereby disclaims any responsibility for them.

Writers' Branding
1800-608-6550
www.writersbranding.com
orders@writersbranding.com

CONTENTS

About the Author
The Real Story of Ear-Wick
The Miracle of now Sally
The Master's Journey
The Boy's Voice for Freedom
At the Master's Feet

I dedicate this book to my wife and our families.

ABOUT THE AUTHOR

Leo R. Hunt had a happy childhood born in Nebraska. His father moved his family to Idaho Spring Colorado. The story that was told about the trip in a secondhand Dodge Van with his wife and three children and a goat. The reason for the goat was because Leo was allergic to cow's milk. When they reached Idaho Spring, his father worked in a gold mine for his brother-in-law. The gold ran out that his father moved his family to Dumont Colorado where they lived in a log cabin were the lady that wrote God Bless America lived.

Leo started his education in a one room schoolhouse then when jobs were no longer available Abe moved his growing family to Dillon Colorado and went to work on one of the largest dams in Colorado. When the dam was finished, the family moved to Denver Colorado. Leo attended three school in North Denver: Smedley Elementary, Horace Man junior high and North high. Leo struggled his entire life with poor grades, spelling and math because of his severe dyslexia. Back in the day, the teachers knew nothing about this disease. They just assumed that the child was slow and move the student from grade to grade. Leo did not start to write his poetry until he was in his twenty's. He explained it this way. "One day the words started coming to me I grabbed a piece of paper and began to write them down however it was a real struggle because of my dyslexia." Finally he meets a woman that could decipher his handwriting and she made his works come a live. He self-published his first book Inspired in 2010 after the book was publish, he begins to write again this time it was much easier because of the computer.

Scattered to the Wind is much different then Inspired however there are some of the old in the new. This is the first attempt for him to write stories, but he feels he has something to say and hope people will like the stories.

A Special thanks to my editor

Mrs. Janene Hunt

A Special thanks to Gotcha Secretarial Service

Thanks to a great guy for all his help

Computer tech

Bob Carter

I want to say great artwork to a great woman

Gail Heil

To all of you my very best wishes for wealth, health, and happiness

And may God bless you all.

THE REAL STORY OF THE EAR-WICK

CHAPTER 1

Abraham F. Hunt lived in a small village on the east shore of England. Abe as he was known was the headmaster of Northern High school. He was in his second year at this position in 1881. He met and fell in love and married with Ruth Alice Delmont.

A year and a half later they had their first child and named him after his grandfather. As Bryan grew, Abe detected that his son had a gift for learning. Abe began to home school him at three months. He started with simple words like mom, cat, dog by the fifth month Bryan was talking and by the age of six-month Bryan could care on a conversation.

Abe's major was anthropology Abe began to read to Bryan his passion showing Bryan some picture of the digs, he helps uncover much to Abe surprise Bryan began to show interest.

Bryan excels in school at the age of fourteen. He graduated from high school. Abe asked Bryan if he wanted to go to Oxford University Oxford because it was his Alma mater.

Abe picked up a pin and paper to write the headmaster of Oxford university asking if he could enroll his young son in the University. Bryan was so excited to think he was going to Oxford.

Each day Bryan would sit on the front porch waiting for the mail to come. Several days passed, Bryan began to worry that the headmaster would not reply. One morning, Bryan had his breakfast. He slowly walked out to the front porch and when he looked out the door, the mail man was putting a letter into the mailbox.

Bryan ran to the mailbox then back to the house into the kitchen where his father was sitting, he handed the letter to his father.

"It's here the letter from Oxford."

His father opened the letter as Bryan stood by him patiently.

Abe unfolded the paper and began to read the letter aloud. "Mister Hunt" It began "I am in receipt of you letter inquiry about enrolling your young son in our university. We would love to have him join us however: he is too young to stay in the dorms Please advise."

Bryan heart skipped a beat a large frown crossed his face he slumped into the chair next to his father.

His father chuckled his words were soft.

"Don't worry son. I have the answer."

A big smile came across Bryan's face when his farther picked up his pen an began to write as he spoke "I'll write your aunt and ask her if you may say with her and her husband."

Janice and her husband Kent lived in Oxford about a mile from the university. Abe explained the situation in the letter to Janice then mailed the letter.

Several days passed there was no reply to the letter again Bryan would set on the front porch waiting for the postman as before Bryan worried that that she would not want him to stay with her and her husband. The weekend was over Monday morning came Bryan sat on the front porch waiting when all the sudden he header the sound of the mail truck the truck pulled up to the mailbox Bryan snatched the letter from the postman ran for the house again Bryan stood by his father's side waiting for his father to read the letter.

CHAPTER 2

The second year Bryan was notified that he could stay in the dorms, he was assigned to a room his roommate was a boy about his age. He was a black African boy.

Bryan and his uncle were the first to arrive and beginning putting Bryan things in their place when the door swung open a tall black young man about his age came into the room, took off his hat and in a very loud and confident voice announced.

"My name is Victor; I am from a small fishing village on the Southeast shore of Africa named Kokan my father is the headmaster of Kokan high school."

Both Bryan and his uncle smiled, then Bryan stepped up beside his uncle in a loud confident voice announced.

"My name is Bryan I am from a small fishing village on the Northeast shore of England. My father is the headmaster at the Northern high school."

They all began to laugh from then on Bryan and Victor were very good friends.

Both Bryan and Victor had their goals set in their minds. They both studied very hard.

Their majors were anthropology, they took several trips through out the world working on digs, gaining knowledge and honing their skills.

After four years of hard work, graduation came. The two celebrated until the sun came up.

When they awoke a little after noon they went to lunch and talked about their future.

Victor talked about home and how he was going back to his hometown to teach the young children and become like his father. Bryan sat for a moment, then told of his plans how he wanted to continue his dream of becoming a teacher, but first he wanted to continue his education and travel. They vowed to keep in touch.

CHAPTER 3

Bryan applied for and received an associate position at the university, after several weeks at home he returned to the university and resumed his duties. This position took him all over the world working on digs and writing papers. He published them for the university.

In his second year he was invited by the Chinese government to explore upper Mongolia. In his third week Bryan was exploring some foothills and came upon a clay jar, he began to dig he uncovered several more. As the dig continued and time went on a city emerged that dated back several million years. Bryan named the city Elisabeth Town after his Queen. When he returned to the university he was offered and took the job as head of the Anthropology department.

When Queen Elizabeth heard the news of the discovery and that it was named after her, she summons Bryan to the Castle while he was there the queen knighted him by saying, "From this day forth you will be called Sir Bryan of Elisabeth Town."

Several years had passed one blustery winter day Sir Bryan was sitting at his desk opening his mail when he came across a letter from Victor, he quickly opened it.

"Dear Bryan" It began

"Come quickly there has been a new tribe discovered up country we should explore it.

Victor"

Sir Bryan picked up his pen and began to reply.

"Victor,

As it has happened my winter semester has just ended, I will book passage on the first ship hope to see you in about two weeks." Sir Bryan booked passage to Africa that very day.

The ship was very slow, Sir Bryan took advantage of this time to start his book on Elisabeth Town. While working on his book the time past quicker before he knew it, they were docking. Sir Bryan gathered his belongings, put them in his garment bag went to the front of the ship to disembark.

When he reached the dock, he began to look for Victor. He looked down the dock there was Victor running towards him at full speed.

Victor jumped into Sir Bryans arms then he stepped back, took off his hat, curtsied in a loud voice said,

"Welcome Sir Bryan"

They both laughed then with a burst of words Victor started to tell Sir Bryan about the journey they were about to take to explore the new tribe, but he was talking so fast Sir Bryan held up his hand.

"Victor please slow down I can't understand a word you're saying."

Victor stopped, took a deep breath and started again, He explained to Sir Bryan that he had hired a boat and crew to take them on their journey and that he had purchased all the supply they would need.

CHAPTER 4

When they reached the dock, the captain was standing on the deck and motioned for them to come aboard. As soon as they we aboard the boat started to move, Victor handed the captain a map showing him where they were going. The boat pulled out into the river then the boat lunged forward. Victor joined Sir Bryan on the bow of the boat and began to outline the trip.

Victor explained to Sir Bryan that the trip would take about four days in about one hundred miles they were to watch the shoreline for a river that flowed into this one. It may be very hard to see because of over grow, however the captain was aware and has alerted the crew.

The boat chugged along, Victor and Sir Bryan were very restless, each morning they would stand on the bow of the boat watching the shoreline. On the morning of the fourth day Sir Bryan was awaken by a loud noise in the kitchen.

He got dressed climbed the ladder to the upper deck he was about to pour himself a cup of coffee when he heard one the crew yell out the captain respond to the crew man.

The boat slowed, Sir Bryan dropped his coffee cup ran to the bow of the ship, Victor was already there when he saw Sir Bryan coming toward him, he pointed to the shore.

When Sir Bryan reached Victor's side, he looked where Victor was pointing Victor explained that there was water flowing from under the trees. This was the river they needed to take to find the village that has been discovered. The captain turned the boat into where the water was coming from and pulled into the trees that were hiding the mouth of the river.

The crew started to cut the branches away, as the branches fell you could see the opening getting larger soon the opening was big enough for the boat to get through.

The captain pushed the throttle forward the boat slid into the opening with ease. Victor and Sir Bryan danced around the deck like two children.

Victor ran to the captain and asked him how long it was going to take to get to the cove, the captain looked up at the clock and replied about two hours. Victor rushed out to the bow of the boat where Sir Bryan was standing and relayed the message to him.

They rushed to their cabins, stuffed their belongings into their back packs, when Victor had finished, he rushed back on deck.

They had traveled about two hours, Sir Bryan finished packing claimed the latter to the upper deck, just before he reached Victor, something caught his eye out in the river. He stopped to look there was a small boy swimming for his life not far behind him was a big alligator heading straight for the young boy. Without think, Sir Bryan grabbed his knife from its case at his side, thrust the knife between his teeth, dove into the water swam with all his might.

Now it was a race to see if he could get to the alligator before it reached the young! boy.

Just as the gator was about to lung at the young boy Sir Bryan crawled up the gators back, took his knife from between his teeth and drove it hard into the gators stomach.

The gator began to roll over and over with Sir Bryan on his back and Sir Bryan hanging on for dear life, then the gator went limp, Sir Bryan surfaced and swam for the shore.

He came up out of the river right next to the young boy, the young boy was exhausted still breathing hard but alive.

The boat pulled up onto the shore Victor jumped from the boat rushed to Sir Bryan's side knelled down out of breath he asked Sir Bryan.

"Are you OK."

Sir Bryan was breathing very hard unable to speak but shook his head yes. Sir Bryan lies quiet until he was able to speak turned to Victor.

"There is a very large man standing on the bank with a very large spear." Victor turned to see the biggest black African he had ever seen turned to Sir Bryan and whispered,

"I'll try to speak to him before he decides to use that spear."

Victor was a student of African language he began to use them, however none of them seemed to work. Victor turned to Sir Bryan with a sad look on his face he whispered.

"I have used all but one of the languages I know if this one doesn't work, I am afraid we are sunk."

Victor turned back to the big man in his last attempt to communicate he used the last language he knew. A big smile came on the big man's face, his hand that held the spear drop to his side in his own language replied.

Sir Bryan tapped Victor on the shoulder. "What did you ask him?"

Victor turned to Sir Bryan in a soft voice he relayed what the big man said.

"I asked him his name he is called Mutombo; he is the chief of a tribe on the other side of the mountain. The boy you saved is Kono the boy is his son; he has invited us to come to his village and they will have a big feast in your honor."

Sir Bryan sat for a moment then replied in the same soft voice, "Do you think we should go?"

Victor looked at the chief then back at Sir Bryan. "I think he would be offended if we declined." They both stood up Victor spoke to the chief in his language told him that they would be honored to join him.

The chief turned, picked up his son placed him on his back raised his spear pointed it into the jungle all the men fell in line behind him.

CHAPTER 5

As they continued into the jungle it became overgrown, the sun almost disappeared just leaving enough light to see the path.

They came to a crossroad in the path the chief again raised his spear, pointed to the path he wanted to take when they were about one-half mile on that path, they began to hear a roar, as they continued the roar got louder and louder. The path narrowed the roar was so loud they could no longer talk to one another. When they reached the top of a big hill they could see where the roar was coming from, it was the largest waterfall either one of them had ever seen.

The chief stopped beside the falls, turned looked over the valley then turned and disappeared behind the water, one by one the tribesman followed him. Victor stopped turned, look at Sir Bryan shrug his shoulders then he too disappeared behind the water; Sir Bryan followed.

The cave was very damp and cold, they could barely see the man in front of them. They walked what seemed to be hours but in truth it was about thirty minutes. The cave made a right turn they could see a small light; it brought a smile to both Victor and Sir Bryan. They walked about ten minutes than out into the sun light. They both stopped took a deep breath in amendment they looked out over a large, lush valley. They could see mountains, planes, blue skies, beautiful green trees and beautiful flowers on the hillside and hundreds of great birds in the sky.

Then they heard one of the tribesmen calling to them, they turned they ran to catch up.

As they walked down the mountain they were in awe of the beauty and the peace that you could feel in the air. They walked for about two hours when they began to hear drums off in the distance, the further they walked the louder and faster the drums beat. When they reached the top of the hill, they could see the village at the end of the valley. It was framed in lush green trees a largest shimmering waterfall the grass huts shined in the sunlight like diamond the clear blue sky made it a portrait.

When they reached the path that led down the center of the village, the chief stopped, raised his spear then led the group down the path to a large grass hut that was covered in flowers. When the chief stepped on to the path the entire village started to sing, it was so beautiful it sent shivers down Sir Bryan's spine the singing lasted until the chief sat down on his throne.

When the chief sat down on his throne all the people fell to their knees and bowed in respect, he picked up his son held him high in the air before the crowd.

Then in a loud strong voice the chief proclaimed that today is a holiday that this man saved his son from death there will be a grand feast. He gave the order to begin.

Victor and Sir Bryan were shown to a grass hut where they were given a cool cup of water and chairs to sit on the young woman spoke to Victor in their native tongue, telling him they should rest for the feast will last all night she turned and was gone.

Victor turned to Sir Bryan told him what the young women said they both flopped into the chairs the next thing they knew the young women was back urging them to awaken and to fellow her they both struggled to their feet straightened their close and followed her to the throne where the chief already had a cup at his lips when he saw Victor and Sir Bryan, he motioned them to join him there on his throne motioned Victor to set on one side and for Sir Bryan to set on the other. When they were both seated the chief raised his hand, they were flooded with people bringing them food and drink, the drums began to beat the young women in the very colorfully dresses began to dance the men with their fire torches danced among them. It was almost sunrise before the drum's stopped the people disappeared into their huts.

CHAPTER 6

Victor was awakened by a young boy urging him to come to follow him Victor sat up and noticed he had a brightly color cloth wrapped around his head he looked over at Sir Bryan he too had the same type of cloth on his head he reached over touched Sir Bryan on his shoulder when he awoke Victor showed Sir Bryan the cloth, where upon Sir Bryan reached up took the cloth from his head, they both laugh.

They dressed and followed the young boy out to where several tribesmen were standing, the head of the party stepped out confronted Victor and proceed to tell him that this is a hunting party that they were inviting both to join them without a reply they were handed spears. Victor turned to Sir Bryan relayed the message to him but before Sir Bryan could reply they were pushed out into the tall grass as they cheeped through the tall grass Sir Bryan whispered to Victor that he had a bad feeling about this he thought they must turn about that time a large bore hog hit Sir Bryan from behind Sir Bryan flew high into the air came down hard on the back of the hog the hog again tossed Sir Bryan high into the air this time he came down hard on the hard ground knocking Sir Bryan out cold.

Sir Bryan was cut in several place, but Victor could not see any broken bones they took him back to the grass hut the women came to Sir Bryan's aid with a tar color substance put it on Sir Bryan's wounds.

When Sir Bryan came to, he looked thou hazy eyes at his friend Victor who was asking him if he was OK Sir Bryan tried to speak but the words would not come out of his mouth. The next morning when they awoke Victor came over to Sir Bryan knelled down in a soft voice whispered.

"How do you feel?"

When Sir Bryan's eyes open, he began to laugh and pointed to Victor with the brightly color cloth on his head.

"You sure look cute in your head dress"

They both laughed Sir Bryan sat up slowly looked around. "How long have I been out"

Victor patted him on the shoulder

"Just overnight do you think you can walk"

With Victor's help Sir Bryan got to his feet took a step then dropped his hand from Victor's arm then took another step turned to Victor in a strong voice replayed.

"You know I think I'll be fine"

The sun was very bright, they both shaded their eyes until they reached the chief setting on his thrown.

Victor explained to the chief that Sir Bryan was all right and they will be leaving the following morning the chief shook both of their hand's he told Victor that he would send three of his best men to guide them to the cave, then Sir Bryan ask Victor to ask the chief for some of the substance that the women put on his wounds and told him to thank him the substance worked very well the chief agreed.

The day was spent packing their belonging thank the people for all their help. The evening came quickly, as they were getting ready to go to sleep a young woman stepped into the hut handing both the brightly color cloth as Victor took the cloth, he asked the young women what it was in their custom that they wore the head wrap. Was it to help make you sleep or maybe it would give the person wearing it sweet dreams, then the young women stopped Victor "no no" she said then she began to explain that the head dress must cover the ears to prevent the Ear-Wick from intering your ear if the Ear-Wick entered the ear it would go to sleep for ten days then when it awoke it would be very hunger and start to eat its way, through your head to the other ear if it were not caught it would turn around and start back.

Victor turned to Sir Bryan and told him what the young women said, as Victor wrapped the cloth around his head Sir Bryan laughed tossed the cloth on the ground explaining to Victor that it was a tribal myth there was no truth to the story he chuckled as he lay on the mat on the dirt floor then fell asleep.

The next morning, they said their goodbyes to the chief and to all the tribe. The three-tribesman started out and Victor and Sir Bryan fell in behind them.

CHAPTER 7

After about three hours they came to the path that led to the cave as they began their assent, they heard the growling of a leopard but could not see it in the tall grass. The tribesman raised their spears pointed to the path that would take than to the cave. When all the sudden a large leopard jumped from the tall grass landing on Victor's back driving his claws deep into Victor's back Victor screaming in pain, he fell to the grown with the leopard on top of him the tribesmen quickly drove their spears into the leopard the leopard fell from Victor's back was dead on the ground.

Victor was awake Sir Bryan ask if he wanted to return to the Villager or could he make it to the boat. Victor manages to tell Sir Bryan to get him to the nearest hospital, so Sir Bryan applied some of the substance that the women used on his wounds then applied it to Victor's back hopping it would help to relive the pain.

The tribesman made a stretcher put Victor on it when they reached the boat Victor thanked the tribesmen the boat pushed off.

When they pulled up to the dock there as an ambulance waiting, they rushed Victor to the hospital. Several days passed finely Victor was awake Sir Bryan rushed to his side told Victory how happy he was to see that he was going to be OK.

CHAPTER 8

They sat and talked about the trip, until visiting hour was over, the hospital had provided a room for Sir Bryan so that he may be close to his friend.

Sir Bryan left Victor as he was walking back to his room, he had a sharp pain in his head but by the time he reached his room the pain was gone, and he dismissed it.

Sir Bryan was fast asleep when the sharp pained returned it was so severe that it woke him up, he screamed in agony the pain was worse than before he cried out for someone to help him.

A doctor down the hall heard the screams then rushed down the corridor to the room where the cries for help was coming from but by the time the doctor got to the room the pain was gone and Sir Bryan was setting up in his bed sweat rolling down his face his eyes full of tears.

The doctor asks Sir Bryan how he could help, Sir Bryan told the doctor of the severe pain in his head, it seems to come about ever fifteen minutes. The doctor told Sir Bryan that he would start running a series of test to see if they could find the reason for the pain.

The days went on the pain seemed to intensify, each time Sir Bryan thought he would go out of his mind. When they had completed all the test the doctor reported back to Sir Bryan.

The doctor walked into Sir Bryan's room carrying several papers in his hand stopped beside Victor who was visiting.

The doctor looked down at the papers then looked up to Sir Bryan

"I am sorry to inform you that after all the testing we are unable to determine the souse of your pain, so I took it upon myself to contact Doctor Robert Allen he is a specialist on this type of head pain.

The next day Doctor Allen came in and visited with Sir Bryan asking him a series of question one of which was have you been up country in the last ten days of course Sir Bryan answered yes.

The doctor investigated Sir Bryan's ears took some samples of tissue stepped back and looked down at "Sir Bryan I am going to have to run some test however I'll get back to you in about thirty minutes."

Thirdly minutes later Dr Allen stepped into Sir Bryan's room walked to the side of the bed looked down at Sir Bryan and in a soft but firm voice

"Sir Bryan I took some samples from your ear; it looks like my suspicions has been confirmed you have and Ear Wick in your head by my calculations the Ear Wick is about halfway thru the journey to your other ear."

Sir Bryan interrupted the doctor.

"Can you give me something for the pain"

The Doctor shuffled the papers in his hand and continued.

"Unfortunately, I cannot if I give you something that will make you sleep the Ear Wick will also go to sleep when it awakes it's going to delay its arrival. at your other ear."

He again shuffled the paper he held in his hands then continued

"In ten days, the Ear Wick will arrive at your other ear, I will have to be right here at that moment to capture the creature when it appears so it will not turm around and make a return trip."

The doctor stood for a moment then turned and lift the room.

Sir Bryan laid there waiting for the next horrific pain to return he would try to brace himself for its arrival but no matter how he would prepare himself it would catch him off guard and he would scream for it to stop.

Ten days had pasted when Doctor Allen returned, he stopped at Sir Bryan's bedside quietly asking how he was doing however Sir Bryan was too weak to answer. The doctor gave him a genital smile then began to explain what was about to happen.

The doctor's voice was strong but firm. "As I have explained you are going to have to lie very still as soon as I have captured this creature, I will rush to the lab examine it to make sure it has no viruses", the waiting began.

The hours past the pain continued the doctor kept his vigilant then from out of the silence came a soft voice the doctor whispered

"It is all most here."

The moments ticked by when suddenly the doctor exclaimed, "I have it"

The doctor jumped from his perch ran for the lab.

Several minutes passed and the doctor had not returned in a week, voice Sir Bryan ask Victor.

"Where is the doctor" just as he spoke, the door opened the doctor slow entered the room he stopped at Sir Bryan bed side again shuffle the papers in his hand in a soft sad voice he spoke "I am afraid I have some good news and some bad news. The good news the worm had no viruses" his voice was soft, the words came out slowly "The worm was a female it has laid an egg in about the center of your head in one week it will hatch, it will be very hungry."

Victor grabbed Sir Brands arm as Sir Bryan grown his eyes filled with tears the doctor patted Sir Brands arm then turned and left the room.

The beginning

THE MIRACLE OF NOW SALLY

Now sally was thrust into this world onto an ice-covered sidewalk, her mother a crack attic lay dying on the frozen sidewalk as she gave birth to a baby girl.

The baby would have followed her mother in death if it were not for the fast thinking of Robert A Hunt badge 1774 who was stopped at the light at fourth and main when out of the corner of his eye, he saw movement he turns his head. He saw a woman falling to the ice-covered sidewalk he leaped from his patrol car but by the time he got to the woman she was giving birth just seconds after the birth she passed away.

Robert quickly took his coat off grabbed the baby girl wrapped the coat around her rushed to his patrol car. He lay the baby girl down on the passenger seat flipped on his siren then rushed her to the hospital.

Now Sally was a small child born with an addiction that made her beginning to live a hard and argues journey. After several heath plagued mounts in the hospital a call was made to the department of human services that they could come and pick up this tiny baby girl.

Several hours passed as the sun was low in the sky a large woman with hairy arms stood at the door of the nursery station the nameless tiny little girl was delivered to her.

The large woman took the baby girl to a large brown stone in the lower part of the city placed her in an unkempt crib with dirty sheet torn baby night gown a long side several small babies. There she would stay for years on end fed twice a day and changed ever so often no madder how hard she cried.

Now Sally had no real contact with other children until she was too big for her crib. The heavy-set woman picked her up put her in a large room with several other children. They ranged in age from five to twelve they were all unkempt with dirty clothes and bodies that had not been washed in a long while. The older children would pick on the small one Now Sally became one of their favorite targets they would wake her up in the middle of the night and make her work for them. One morning two older boys grabbed her, pushed her to the floor, held her down, the third boy pullered off her pants and was about to rape her the large woman, heared the screams from the big room. She burst through the door grabbing the three boys and drug them off. Now Sally would stay in the big room for two years never to get out of this honorable place until one morning the large woman came into the big room grabbed Now Sally took her off to the kitchen set her down at a table across from a large black woman. Mabel as she was known was worked too hard and underpaid, so she took it out on the children. Mabel set for a moment looking at this tiny child as the hairy armed woman was leaving Mabel's last words came out at a diffing volume. "I ask for help and this is what you bring me" Mabel sat for a moment just looking at Now Sally then at the same volume she begins to shout orders to her tiny helper. "Grab that bucket full of soap and water and start washing the floor. Now Sally slipped from her chair walked to the bucket turned to look at Mable. Mable's angery voice came at a frightening volume. "What's a matter child don't you know how to wash the floor" Now Sally with her head bowed in shame she shook her head no. Mable got up from her chair walked over to Now Sally grabbed the rag from the bucket flipped water all over Now Sally and the floor then began to scrub the floor.

Mable stopped through the rag at Now Sally knocking her to the floor Mable's loud voice again shattered the silence "Now get up and do as your told" At midday Mable sat down at the table called to Now Sally to come to lunch.

Now Sally rushed to the table climbed up on her chair much to her surprise there was one carrot, but she was so hungry she grabbed it and ate it so fast it nearly choked her. At the end of the day Mabel took

Now Sally to a big brown door open it pushed her inside and slammed the door. The room had no light except for the light that came thru a dingy window that was so far up she could not see out of it.

Now Sally was very frightened however she was so tired she lay down on some rags on the floor and fell asleep.

The darkness closed in on this tiny little girl then the devil took her from peaceful sleep to searing pain between her large the pain was so great she could hardly breath the pain lasted most of the night when morning came the door open, Mable stood as a large shadow in the blinding light her loud harsh voice rain down on Now Sally like a terrifying lighting storm calling her to get up and get to scrubbing the floor. When the day was done Mable grabbed Now Sally and drug her to the big brown door open it and pusher her inside. Now Sally was so terrified she curled up in the corner of the small room then sleep took her from her fear, the night passed, the pain let her sleep-in peace. Another night passed the pain did not disturb her sleep however the third night the pain snatched her from her sleep the pain through her body like a red-hot sword she started to scream when a large smelly hand cover, her tiny mouth and she fell unconscious.

Each night he would come and cascades his lust over this tiny girl.

As the years passed Now Sally retreated within herself her mind would close out everything around her, she found a friend there in the darkness they would walk and play together for hours even as she worked the day, through.

One day she was walking past a door there was a fresh smell coming from the unlocked door. She pushed on the door; the door swung open to a new world a world she had never seen. She had never been outside and did not even know it existed she stepped out on to something green however she had no name for it. Now Sally was never educated and only knew the words that Mable spoke to her.

She walks through a gate starts down the street her uneducated mind was now at war with her surrounding she could not understand all that was about her, she saw all the bright color thing going past her but did not know what they were, nor did she know they could harm her. She stepped into the street one of brightly colored thing came to screeching halt she screams when all at once two strong arms wrapped around her, scooped her up, put her back on the sidewalk little did officer Robert Hunt know that twelve years ago he had picked this same little girl off the sidewalk and rushed her to the hospital.

'What is your name "Officer Robert asks in a soft voice not to frighten this tiny girl a moment passed she replayed in a voice that reeked of pain "Now Sally" Officer Robert stunned with her reply tried to continue the conversation again in a soft voice. "Where do you live" A blank look covers Now Sally face she had never heard those words, so, she had no answer for him. Officer Robert did not further the conversation pick up his phone called health and human service. About ten minutes later nurse Janene stopped her car beside officer Robert as soon as she saw this tiny little girl with her dirty face and torn clothes, her heart when out to her. Nurse Janene Slowly got out of her car and very quietly approached office Robert, she introduced herself then kneeled down to speak with this poor neglected child then with her most present voice.

"Hi, My Name, is Janene what's your name" A faded smiled cross this tiny little girl lips and her voice as soft as a breeze floated in the air. "Now Sally" With surprise looked on her face Janene look up at officer Robert and smiled office Robert smiled and shrugged his shoulder. Nurse Janene thanked office Robert picked up Now Sally put her in the back seat of her car reached for the seat belt started to pull the belt across Now Sally's lap. Memory flashed a cross Now Sally foggy mind of a dark room and being held down she began to scream as the pain flashed across her body.

Janene picked her up and began to consul her when Now Sally regained her peace Janene asked office Robert if he would drive her to her home, she would hold Now Sally on her lap in the back seat. Janene carried Now Sally into the house set her down on her bed went into the bathroom turned the water into the tub then walked into another room. Now Sally set in awe of how bright the room was and how soft the bed was she had never seen anything like this. Janene walked back into the bedroom with an arm full of clothes from a little girl that was her little girl long time passed.

Janene took off the raggedy clothes picked up Now sally carried her into the bathroom gently lowered her into the warm water Now Sally stiffened not ever have had this feeling before but once in the water she felt it's warmth then she relaxed, Janene began to bath her. Once the bath was over Janene carried Now Sally into the bedroom gently lowered her onto the bed then began to dress her when she was all dressed Janene picked her up placed her in front of the floor mirror Now Sally had never seen her reflation before she smiled then began to laugh and dance like she did with her friend.

The next morning Janene was dressing Now Sally and ask her where she got her name. Now Sally looked up at Janene with a sigh as if Janene should know. "It was Mable where I lived before, she would always say Now Sally wash the floor Now sally wash the dishes." Janene choked down her laughter Janene picked up Now Sally carried her to the car open the door sat her down in the back seat then started to put the seat belt over her Now Sally stiffen then Janene assured her it would be ok. Once in Janene office Janene sat Now Sally on a chair Janene began to fill out the forms to place Now Sally into foster care, when she started to fill out the name on the form she stopped and turned to Now Sally her voice present and sweet she began. "This may be hard for you to understand" Janene explained

"We are going to change your name to Sally Hunt because officer Roberts last name is Hunt, and he is as close to a relative you have"

Sally smiled, Janene continued to fill out the form when she was finished, she stood up looked at Sally grabbed the papers she had been writing on told Sally she would be right back then left the room. Sally set there wondering if she was going to be sent back to where she lived before. Janene rushed into the room with a big smile on her face she picked up Sally gave her a big hug then with an all most crying whisper she announced.

"They gave me you I am going to be your mother now your name is Sally Hunt Floman."

Janene could no longer hold back the tears of happiness Sally did not fully understand it, but she knew that Janene was happy she felt safe now and she gave her mother a big kiss on the cheek Sally life has been changed forever more.

A new beginning

THE MASTERS JOURNEY

The Master on his journey came across a boy sitting on a boulder staring into a deep pool in the river. The Master stopped watched the boy for a moment then in a soft voice not to startle the. Young boy his words seemed to float on a sunbeam the boy turned. "What is it that you are looking for in that deep pool?" The Master asks.

The boy turned gazed upon the Master for a moment. Then his words came as a gust of wind from a lofty tree. Are my toughts not words?

"Are my eyes not seeing my future? Are my dreams Not real? To whom can I speak to make my life whole"?

Then the flow of words went silent, the boy sat back on the rock waiting for the answer to his questions.

The Master stood for a moment in deep thoughts searching his mind for the right answer to the boy's question.

A wide smile quivered over the master's lips Then disappeared. The Master gazed into the boy's eyes: his word came softly at first but as the words came clear in his mind the volume began to grow.

"Your creator has guided you on your Path now it is you that must take the next step. Your Mother and Father have taught you the value of truth now you must look within yourself follow truth walk that path. When you see a dove leave the branch do you ask where it is going or do you watch and known that it his mind that guides him.

Our creator asks that you listen before you speak. If the words you speak are not true let them never leave your lips. Ask for blessing for others before you ask for yourself. Use your voice to guide your neighbors and your family be true to yourself, then you will know your truth."

"Please sir tell me more about how-to live-in life."

The Master sat on the ground the boy jumped from his perch then set beside the Master. The Master sat for a time watching the clouds in the sky drift a long their way, then in a mellow voice the words seem to come from the clouds.

"Each of us has their own beginning their own path and their own dreams."

You have used your eyes to see your dreams follow the dreams you have created in your heart and mind. You have truth in your heart, listen to the song that dwells within make that path your path. The Master looked to the river and pointed to its flow, "See how the river flows, it is like live itself, it takes the bend with ease and if it comes to a boulder, its flows over or around it without cause to ask why it is there.

Life is as the river; you are the flow. Even the river flows to become something greater than itself as it reaches the sea, you must guide yourself become part of humanity make your life a pattern that the people will follow.

The Master stood to continue his journey, he turned to the young boy gaze into his eyes as a small smile repelled across his lips then he looked to the path he must take he went on his way. The boy, becoming a young man stood watched until the Master had disappeared around the bend, his heart and mind was filled with the master's words the words give him the strength to go fourth and live his life. The boy walked a few steps then turned once again, to see where the Master had stood wondering if he would ever see him again.

As he walked down the path a smiled crossed his lips and joy filled his heart. Filled with the master's words he knew in his heart that he could live in peace.

The beginning of a new life.

THE BOY'S VOICE FOR FREEDOM

Recalling memory of a place now forgotten, a baby boy orphaned at birth lived in a small town in Pintola. He was named by the midwife Ohan, meaning (peace to county). The midwife took the baby boy to an orphanage, then left him as a ward of the state. The orphanage was overcrowded, and the children were made to work for their food. If they did not do their work satisfactory, their food was withheld for a full day.

If there was a second offense, they were sent to the barn where they were put in a room without light. The children called the room hell-of-darkness. From the moment that Ohan was able to think for himself, he knew he had to escape this living hell. One morning Ohan was awakened by a large hand pulling him from his bunk; he was then drug outside, a rope tied around his neck then attached to a cart the master jumped in the cart whipped the horse to a gallop Ohan was made to run all the way to the city.

Once in the city, the master untied the rope from the cart, then pulled Ohan from shop to shop while piling all the supplies on Ohan. When the master was finished shopping, the master returned to the cart, tied the rope to the cart then left for the cafe.

Ohan could not believe how poor and hungry the people were. He knew then what he had to do. He must escape to free the people from this tyranny. Ohan watched the master. When he was out of sight, Ohan started to loosen the rope from around his neck. The sun was very hot, so Ohan crawled under the cart, then continued to loosen the knot. Suddenly, the rope was jerked up pulling Ohan to his feet. The master's voice was loud and harsh as he jumped into the cart, whipped up the horse to a gallop with Ohan running behind.

Several days later, Ohan was sitting at the lunch table with several of the other boys when a guard came to the table, ordered all the boys at the table to follow him. All the boys stood up, then followed the guard. When they got to the door, the guards put a rope around the neck of each boy; the door opened, they were led out to a wagon told to get aboard. Ohan leaped up on the wagon then turned to help the younger boys onto the wagon. All the sudden the wagon jerked forward one of the smaller boys fell off. Ohan screamed for them to stop, but the wagon continued. The wagon lumbered along for some time, then when they reached the top of a hill, they could see the castle in the distance shimmering in the sunlight.

Now Ohan knew where they were going, he knew he must look for a way to escape. The wagon pulled through the gate, then stopped right in front of the garden. A guard ordered all the boys off the cart. Ohan stood and looked around; he could see a gate to his right. It was about a hundred yards away. He jumped off the wagon landing right in front of one of the guards. The guard yelled at him to get a move on as he ordered all the boys to clean the castle grounds.

Ohan bent over and pretended to be picking things off the ground as he moved towards the gate with one eye on the gate the other one on the guard. He moved closer and closer to the gate. When he could no longer see the guards, he broke out into a fast run. He could see that the gate was locked without slowing down, he leaped high into the air over the gate and into the forest.

Ohan ran for about one hundred yards when he came across a path that would take him south, away from the orphanage. Ohan was tired but he knew that he had to keep running to avoid the guards. The sun was getting lower in the sky. Ohan kept looking for a place to hide for the night. Just as the sun was going down, he could see a barn in the middle of a grove of trees. Ohan got to the barn with enough light to see that the barn had a loft full of hay. He scurried up the ladder, then dove into the hay and fell asleep.

Ohan woke up to a soft voice sing he rubbed his eyes stretch. His body then crawled to the edge of the loft peered over the edge to see a young girl milking her goat.

Ohan thought for a moment on who to contact her without her screaming then before he knew it the words were leaving his lips in a soft voice he said "Hello" the young girl stopped milking her goat turned her head from side to side not seeing anyone she continues to mike her goat. Ohan then tried again in a louder voice "good morning"

The young girl stopped milking her goat, stood up, then turned around. Her voice kind of shrill, showing a little fright, she continued, "Where are you, what do you want, show yourself, stop acting like a thief." Ohan stood up, then leaped from the loft landing on one knee right in front of the girl. He looked up at her, then in a voice that trembled, he began to tell her his story.

Ohan told her when he was ten, the master put a rope around his neck, then made him run all the way to the city, and how he was trying to escape when the master caught him then beat him. And how poor the people were in the village. That made him want to go against the king to get back the people's freedom. He took a deep breath in a more reassuring voice he asked, "I am looking for a friend to help me free the people." Alma studied Ohan's face, then in a compassionate voice she replied "Well, if you stop talking, I will answer your question." She set the bucket of milk down, looked at Ohan, then continued "My Name is Alma. I don't know if I will be your friend. I, however, will get my father, then you can tell your story to him." Alma disappeared out the barn door.

Ohan sat down on a bag of oats, then leaned back against the wall to rest. He was about to close his eyes when he heard footsteps outside the barn. Ohan jumped to his feet, stepped into an empty stall. Alma and her father stepped into the barn and Ohan stepped out of the stall to greet them. Alma looked at her father, in a pleasant voice she spoke to her father. "Father, this is Ohan, the young man I told you about. She turned, looked at Ohan and in the same voice she spoke "Ohan this is Abraham, my father, he would like to hear your story.

Ohan put out his hand then asked Abraham for his blessing as was the custom. Abraham took Ohan's hand and blessed him; their hands dropped to their sides.

They all sat down on the oat sacks, then Ohan repeated the story he had told to Alma. When he had finished, Abraham took a long look at this young man then in a very sincere voice asked Ohan "If you truly want to go against the king, we are with you. The soldiers came in the night took my son. I want him back at all costs. My son was working with a young man named Kim, I want you to meet him." Abraham turned to his daughter then spoke in a commanding voice,

"Go, my child, to Kim's house bring him here but do not tell him of Ohan." Alma disappeared out the barn door.

While Alma was gone, the two men talked of many things. When suddenly, Ohan heard footsteps outside of the barn. he jumped to his feet, then Abraham's voice called to him to be calm. "It is Alma and Kim, don't be afraid." Kim and Alma stepped into the barn upon seeing Ohan, Kim stopped short, then walked over to Abraham, put out his hand to ask him for his blessing. Even before Abraham could give his blessing, Kim turned to face Ohan, his voice full of anger, his volume loud, the questions came "Who is this boy? Where did he come from? Why is he here? Is he a spy?"

Kim's words stopped, but his emotion showed that the anger still dwelled within. Abraham stepped between the two men, his voice soft but commanding. "Kim" he began "Ohan wants to join us to fight against the king. He wants to help the people so they can regain their freedom." Kim's words came in a softer tone as he walked closer to Ohan. "Is it true that you want to go against the king? Just what is it that a small boy like you can do to make the king change his ways?" Ohan stood tall, his word was strong and only one. "Words", he replied. Kim was surprised by Ohan's answer and broke out in a loud laughter as he turned to Abraham and Alma. "Did you hear that he is going to fight the king with Words... Words... Words."

Kim stopped his laughing, whipped around and stood still as if lighting had struck, his face grim, his eyes on fire, the volume of his voice lower but still showing the anger within. "You're a fool! Go back from where you came, take your words with you. I have been fighting the king for several years. I have killed some of his soldiers. He has killed some of our freedom fighters because that's all the king knows.

"Kim turned and started for the barn door when Ohan's words stopped him. "Have you won yet"? Kim stopped, turned around, walked over to Abraham and they all started to laugh. The three of them walked over to Ohan and with their arms open wide, they all embraced. From that day forward, Kim and Ohan were best of friends. Abraham invited all into the house where he made them lunch. They were eating and talking when all the sudden Kim dropped his fork, pointed to Ohan, then exclaimed "Abraham, do you know who this is?" Abraham stopped eating then turned to look at Ohan. "Are you thinking what I am thinking, who he looks like?" His words returned to his lips for it was forbidden to speak his name. Kim moved closer to Ohan and his excitement exploded into words. "It is Salam's son I would bet one of my pigs on it."

Ohan sat still, when his words came, his voice was at a whisper. "Did you know my father? I have heard his name spoken by some slaves." Kim looked about, then spoke in a whisper. "Yes, all people have heard your father's name but the king has forbidden us to speak his name. He was the prophet from the east with truth on his lips. One night he was to speak to the people; however, the king knew the people were listening to him so that night he disappeared, he has not been seen again. There are rumors that he is in the king's prison, but no one knows for sure."

Now all words were spoken in a whisper. Before they spoke, they would look around to make sure no one was listening. Abraham stood up with a puzzled look on his face, his words in a whisper broke the silence. "Where should we hide him?" They all sat quiet until Kim's voice broke the silence. "Your farm in the mountains; the king doesn't even know it is there." They all agreed and began to prepare for the journey.

The next morning, they were up before dawn. The three of them slipped out into the darkness so no one could see them leave. When they reached the trail to start up the mountain, they all looked back over the valley to make sure no one was following them. Satisfied that there was no one behind them, they started up the mountain. It took them three hours to reach the path to the farmhouse.

When they stepped out of the forest, there was a farmhouse sitting at the end of a long valley. There were cows and deer grazing on the lush grass in the meadow. By the time they reached the farmhouse, they were all very tired and slumped into the chairs and sat there until the sun started to fade.

Abraham got up to start a fire in the stove to prepare dinner.

The next morning, Abraham was up early making coffee and cooking breakfast. The men enjoyed a pleasant breakfast. When they were finished, Abraham took the dishes out to the pump, rinsed them off, took them back, placed them in the cupboard. He then went over sat beside Ohan then spoke softly telling Ohan that they were going to leave him here. They would go to the people tell them of their plan. When the time was right, they well tell the people who you are and that they would be returning soon. It would take them about thirty days to reach their goal. When they had reached all the people, they would return for him. Abraham and Kim packed their backpacks then started their return trip. Ohan walked Kim and Abraham to the gate then watched them until they disappeared into the forest.

Ohan spent his days reading taking long walks, getting clear in his mind the words he would say to the people and the king. Time crawled slowly, the hours dragged on, thirty days came and went. Ohan was getting worried that they would not come for him.

One night a voice called to Ohan in his dreams "Ohan" the voice he whispered. Then a figure appeared that looked much like himself and began to speak to him. "I am your father. I am in the king's prison. I need you to take my place with the people. Using the right words, you will capture the hearts of the people, then they will follow you.

Then you can go to king to make him hear the people's story. Tell the king who you are and you have truth in your heart."

Ohan awoke suddenly, got up walked to the front door staring at the spot where his friends would appear. He fixed his meal when he had finished, he walked down to the gate. He would stand there a long while hoping to see his friends step out of the forest. He turned to return to the cabin when he caught a movement out of the corner of his eye, he turned his head to see two figures step out of the forest his heart was filled with joy.

Abraham and Kim came closer, they stopped short as they could not believe what they were seeing. In front of them stood a man full of confidence his demeanor was that of a man who knew of the world was ready to fight for his people. Ohan's face was bearded and his robe was as white as a cloud in a clear blue sky. Ohan raised his hand in a soft but commanding voice he spoke." I have waited for your return. Please come to the house, I will fix a meal then I will tell you of my dream.

After they were finished with their meal Ohan stood up in a soft voice he began to tell of his dream. Ohan's voice was soft at first, however his voice began to raise with the fire that burned within him. "We must stop the killing. We must use the words that the king will listen to. We must get all the people to speak as one voice. When we all speak in one voice, the king will listen. We can start by giving the words to the people by putting articles in the paper. When we are all speaking the same words, we can go to the king.

The first paper hit the streets the people read it, the guards read it, even the king read it. Ohan was surprised there was no reaction to his words; the people waited for the king's wrath but all was still. Monday's paper grew stronger, it read "We the People of this land go hungry, our children are starving and dying because our king is of greed. He has taken our children's life and stolen our happiness. The king will have our lives if we don't stand up and fight for our freedom."

Two days later, another paper came out, then four days later, another article appeared in the paper. Ohan became the voice of the people and the target of the king. You could tell there was hope in the hearts of the people, there were smiles and joy. On the thirteenth day, the paper appeared on the street, the truth of all truth came to the people. The paper came out with the blessing of the priest giving the people the drive to go to the king.

However, the king was silent.

Ohan wrote an article in which he referred to the king as a greedy fool. The king was greedy king; however, he was a smart king he knew that if he had Ohan killed, it would light the fuse, then he would no longer have control. When the king read the article, he screamed, "My laws have been broken now someone must pay." He called his guard, then in a soft voice so only the guard could hear, he whispered. "Bring me the man called Ohan. I want him alive and unharmed."

Three days later Ohan stood before the king. The king sat staring down at Ohan, then the king's voice rained down on Ohan like a thunderstorm. "You are one of the boys from the orphanage where I send food and clothing. Then you turn on me. Well, my friend I am not going to put you in my prison, I am going to set you free to walk anywhere you want in the land of Bastonia." The king broke out in a loud laughter; then all of a sudden the king stop laughing, pointed down at Ohan with the volume of a thunderstorm, screamed "Get him out of my sight." The guards pushed Ohan to the floor and made him to crawl out of the king's chamber as was the custom when a prisoner was exiled. When darkness fell, the guards pulled Ohan out to a wagon threw him in it. The wagon lurched forward into the night.

A lone rider followed the wagon; everyone in the village knew the name of the king's assassin and they knew that he would not return until he had completed his mission. The next morning Kim followed the wagon, he knew that he too would not come back until he could bring Ohan home. The next morning when the village awoke, everyone knew that their voice was gone that they were at the mercy of the king.

The last article appeared in the paper that Ohan had written days before. "Man has broken the law of nature by killing his own kind, peace is on their lips but in their hands are weapons of war. Who will seek vengeance on man for killing his own kind? Why does it make men of power so cruel?"

One year later, Kim found Ohan in an abandon warehouse half alive but so very happy to see Kim. They talked until the sun had gone down, then Kim stood up, told Ohan he would go out to see if he could find some food, then disappeared into the darkness. Ohan leaned back on his pillows was about to fall asleep when a voice came out of the darkness. "Ohan, I have come from your king to wish you pleasant dreams. Do not look at me for I have heard that to look into your eyes is to see the sorrow of a thousand years." Ohan knew the voice of the king assassin; he knew that he would come. Maston stepped out of the darkness; his sword glimmered in the candlelight. Ohan sat still for a time then reached for a club at his side. Maston laughed, his voice had the sound of cruelty his words rained down on Ohan full of hate. "You think that club is a match for my sword?" Maston hovered over Ohan, he raised his sword high over his head, then as he was about to plunge the sword into Ohan's chest there was a large thump came from Maston's head he fell to the floor. Standing behind him was Kim with a large club. Kim stepped into the light with a big smile on his face. "Well, it looks like I got back with the food just in time."

When they had finished eating Kim tied Maston up so they could sleep. The morning came with a cool breeze that came through the broken window. Ohan sat up as did Kim they were quiet for a time, then Ohan's words came as a melodious bell rung by an angel. "I have run into the depths of emptiness. I have hidden in the darkness for time eternal. My words have been trapped in my soul. Before my soul is sent into the emptiness, I wish to speak so that my earth-bound anger is done. Maston, was lying on the floor, but fully awake, his words filled with hate and rage. "Speak, Ohan, but when your words have ceased to flow from your lips, your life will follow them into the emptiness for I am not the only one that left the castle that night."

"Ohan sat for a time, his words came as if there were a lifetime of happiness, joy, pain, and sorrow. Ohan spoke with the age of a hundred years. "The triumphs have been, now only death can be. I have stepped from a dream only to see the end. I want not now that I have given. I cry not for myself but for the job unfinished, I cry for the people I have left in tears." Ohan stood up walked to the broken window took a deep breath then again, his words came as a fresh breeze. "For now, I live without thought; there is not me anymore for I have joined the numbers. I have become as the pebble of sand on the shore of life. I have not forgotten nor can I recall the truth I wish to tell.

I have been set adrift on the sea of reality. I am carried on the tide of humanity." Ohan walked back to the table looked down at the two men. "What is peace, can it be found? Is it high or under the ground? Can it be bought; can it be sold? Is it new or is it old? Can you have it and give part away? Can we live it day by day? Can there be peace without death or dying? Is peace when no one is crying? What is peace? How can it make you feel? Is peace a lover that has run from you? Was I too anxious to be free? Peace and Love, words that people die for. Is the only way to know peace is to fight and die? People die for peace and freedom. Why can't people live for peace and freedom?"

Ohan sat back in his chair and looked out of the broken window as the clouds drifted by. Words swirled in his head, then like a burst of wind from a lofty tree, the words flew from his lips, "The voice of the mighty cover the meek. The strong overshadow the weak. The voice of the meek call but no one comes near. We have forgotten from all there is something to hear. We have forgotten the voice of silence can now be heard. To the loud voice thy will be done. It is the voice of love that will make us as one. Love will come like cool rain then we will sing the song of peace."

Ohan seemed to be in a trance; his words came in a louder voice. "What happened to the sun, did it die? What happened to the clouds, do they cry? Because peace was yesterday. Morning without the sun is darkness, the darkness of hell of life. Because peace was yesterday. When in life, do we give? When in life, do we live? No one can live in darkness, no one can live in light when your eyes are closed to peace. We live in our house without the sun because peace was yesterday."

Ohan turned then looked at Maston, but past him to the king, to his country, to his people, to his judgment of all men. His face tense, his word sharp, his voice half in anger and half in love, "Words without end, the war is over. To whom do we try for the murder of peace? Who is the blame for the genocide against man? Who is guilty? Shall we try the man that did not

go to war sent their fellow man in their place to kill or be killed. The people will set the sentence condemning the people without love for their country. Before we set the sentence and condemn, hear this. We are all guilty. No man who has not spoken out before the killing cannot speak out now. He must stay as a mute until the words of love and peace are on his lips. Your mourning did not stop the dying nor did your tears stop the rape and genocide against your own kind. Because your voice was silent, the killing ran rampant over a distant land, the dying of your kin came back to you tenfold in grief. Just to live is not enough, nor is your dying. Holding back the words of peace are the lives we cannot lose, for without them, peace will not be."

Ohan looked to the eyes of Maston as to say, my words are finished, now my soul is willing to be sent into the emptiness. Maston's heart was filled with love. All the hate had gone. He thought now of life not death. His words were of forgiveness. His voice trembled as he asks Ohan to forgive him, "Please Ohan take me with you wherever you go that I may guard life not take it my words are now of peace." Kim cut the ropes from Maston's body, reached down helped him to his feet and a new life. Ohan, Kim and Maston stood in an embrace, vowing to only speak of love and peace.

Ohan spoke as the fourth one, "Freedom begins with love and we will be free." Ohan walked to the broken window, stood there for a moment, then turned to Kim and Maston, "If your hearts are now at peace, take me back to our village that I may speak to our people." Ohan spoke to the people of, peace without death, freedom without persecution, peace and love for all. The following morning there was a gathering in the village square. They all began to sing the song of peace as they walked to the castle. The king heard the song the people were singing it melted his heart. He walked to the door of the balcony, pushed the door wide open, then stepped onto the balcony with his arms wide open. Ohan stepped out of the crowd with his arms wide open his voice was loud and strong.

"My name is Ohan. I have turned from my father's ways. We are here as your subjects, not your servants, we want to be partners in this land of peace. We will follow your words as long as they are true. We will pay our taxes as long as there is enough for us to live. The king bowed to the crowd the crowd bowed to the king. The people returned to the village with love in their heart and a promise of a new day.

The Beginning

The Gift of Life

AT THE MASTER'S FEET

A young boy sat at the Master feet to learn life's story and he asks the Master

"What of the Wind"

The master sat for a time gazed out the window to the tree and beyond then in a soft voice that gathered volume as he spoke.

"The wind can be fickle it plays in the trees on a warm summer day and move the leaves to its rhythm, or it can become angry and a monster, it can take everything from us that we hold dear. We must watch the clouds they will tell us of the winds mood so that we may prepare for its wrath. We can hide from the wind however when it is angry, it knows no friends." The master sat in his place his voice went silent.

The young boy sat for a time watching the master as a question quivered on his lips before he knew it the words leaped from his lips shattering the silence.

"What of the rain"

The Master leaned to the open door spoke in a soft voice as for the clouds not to hear.

"The rain is a gift from the All Mighty its blessing gives the flowers their life, the grass to grow so the animals of the field have food to make them strong. It gives life to the grain and the oats that we make our bread that will keep us healthy. As the clouds wanders across the fields and the forest it releases it bounty so the wild animals may feast on its glory."

The Master leaned again to the open door watching the clouds come up over the horizon, he began again as he continued to watch the clouds.

"The rain can join the angry wind and overpower us so that we must flee our homes rush to the heights peaks to escape its wrath. When the Wind regain its peace, we again bask in their glory."

The Master once again slipped into his peace closed his eyes to shut out the light.

The young boy watched the Master in his peace choking back the word to his next question that was dancing on his tongue, he tightens his lips to hold the words from jumping out of his mouth, when all at once the words flew out of his mouth with more gusto than before.

"What of the thunder and lightning"

The Master stirred from his peace pointed to the highest peak he spoke in a loud voice as for the peaks to hear.

"The lighting dances across the sky showing it's fury, warning us to be afraid for when it comes to earth it flies on the wings of death. We must leave our homes go to the highest peaks we sheller in the caves to save our lives."

Lowering his gaze to his blanket he slipped once again into his silent. The young boy shy and without experience his lips dry scanned the master's face for a sign that he may ask another question, the master's eyes fluttered, the young boy took it that the Master was ready to hear his question in a soft voice a breeze cared the question to the master.

"What of Love"

A soft chuckle rumbled across the master's lips the words came softly as not to embarrass the young boy. The master rose from his pillows looked into the young boy's eyes, then to the sky as to look for the right answer the words came as a melody to the young boy ears.

"The word Love is as mystical as the moon as distant as the stars and as vast as the universe, you can drown in it or float on it. The question you ask is as old as man himself. Each man has hidden within him his answer. However, before you can answer the question. You must ask who do I love? You see there are many types of love. You love your father and mother for they have brought you into this world raised you and protected you. There for, you love them with a love that comforts you. You love your sister and brother with a love that seals the bond that makes your family whole. You love your dog Rex and your cow Molly you have compassion for them for what they bring to your family. There is a love locked within your heart, there is someone somewhere that has the key that will unlock that love. There is no answer to whom or where the key lies but when that key is put into your heart you will know that your life is complete. Remember love is like a garden it needs equal parts of sunshine and rain; you are the gardener."

The Master leaned back on his pillows his eyes closed but before he could slip into his peace the young boys words came as a bolt from the blue.

"What of God"

The master eyes opened sharply, he looked right through the young boy and up to the sky as to search for the answer to the young boy's question. Then the master leaned back on his pillows still with his eyes looking to the heavens then began to speak.

"Man has searched for the answer to this question from the beginning of time each man has the answer to this question deep within his soul your answer is within you. You must search for the answer that lies in your heart and soul. Even if a man confesses to you that he does not have the power within him, to be better than he is, it is because he has not searched for it, nor does he know how. For no man can live on this earth without the belief that there is a greater power then himself, that power lies within him and when he finds that power his life will be easier, he will live in peace, he will be fulfilled. When it comes to you, your eyes will be his eyes your voice will be his voice you will bask in his glory. Your truth is your path to follow serve other as you serve yourself, give as you are living, show all the passion for your life. There is only a second between truth and lies in that second you must stop ask yourself is this the path he would walk? Then your truth will be known. You will walk the path of truth be a believer in life."

The Master tired from the day leaned onto his pillows his eyes closed slipped into his peace. The young boy sat for a time drinking in the master's words watching the master at peace. The answers to his question have been fulfilled he stood and walked into the fading light down the path to his life.

A Dream Fulfilled

www.ingramcontent.com/pod-product-compliance
Lightning Source LLC
LaVergne TN
LVHW070046070526
838200LV00028B/402